The Planets and the Solar System

Written by Phillip Clarke
Designed by Mike Hill

Contents

The Solar System

Outer planets

Asteroid belt

Inner planets

The Solar System is the Sun and all the planets
and other natural objects that whirl around it.
Its gravity (pulling force) keeps them in their paths.

Note: distances and sizes are not shown to scale.

* **Big Daddy** Without the Sun, the Earth would never have existed. All the planets in the Solar System were formed out of a saucer-shaped cloud of dust and gas that was pulled into shape by the gravity of the infant Sun.

* **Know your planets** To remember the order of the planets in distance from the Sun, try this memory aid: Most (Mercury) Vampires (Venus) Eat (Earth) Moist (Mars) Juicy (Jupiter) Steaks (Saturn) Using (Uranus) Napkins (Neptune).

* **Inner planets** The four planets closest to the Sun are called the inner planets. They are made mainly of rock and metal, have few moons and no Saturn-like rings. Earth is an inner planet.

* **Outer planets** The four outer planets are also called the gas giants. They are at least ten times heavier than Earth, are made mainly of gas, have many moons, and (often faint) rings.

SOLAR SYSTEM FACTS

Diameter: 15 billion km (9.3 billion miles)

Largest planet: Jupiter	**Smallest planet:** Mercury
Fastest planet: Mercury	**Slowest planet:** Neptune
Hottest planet: Venus	**Coldest planet:** Uranus

The Sun

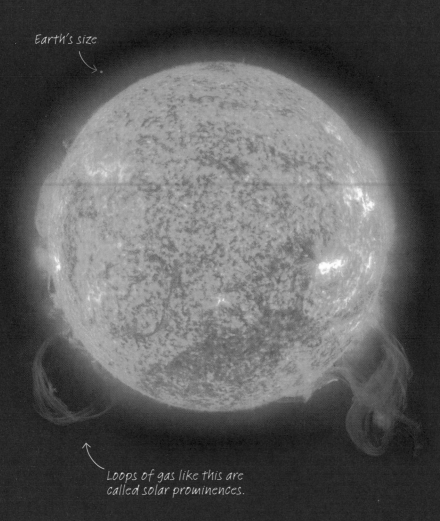

Earth's size

Loops of gas like this are called solar prominences.

The Sun, our closest star, makes up 99.9% of the stuff in the Solar System. This photo filters out the Sun's glare to show its churning surface.

* **Seeing the Sun** The Sun is so bright that staring at it can blind you. But you can look at it safely by projecting its image through a pinhole in one sheet of paper onto another. This is one of the best ways to view a solar eclipse.

* **Yellow dwarf** Compared to other stars, our Sun is fairly bright, medium-sized and middle-aged. It is classed as a G2V star, meaning that it is yellowish-white and in the main sequence or dwarf stage of its life.

* **Sun storms** Dark spots appear on the Sun before it erupts with powerful outbursts called solar storms, shooting out solar flares of plasma (electrically charged gas) or vast coronal mass ejections.

Coronal mass ejection —

* **Dark heart** The heart of the Sun is pitch-black. Invisible rays from the Sun's core take ten million years to reach its surface, where they turn into visible light and beam to Earth in eight minutes.

SUN FACTS

Planets: eight

Diameter: 1.4 million km (870,000 miles)

Adjective: solar

Surface temperature: 5,527 °C (9,981 °F)

Symbol: ☉

Core temperature: 13.6 million °C (24.5 million °F)

Distance from Earth: 150 million km (93 million miles)

Mercury

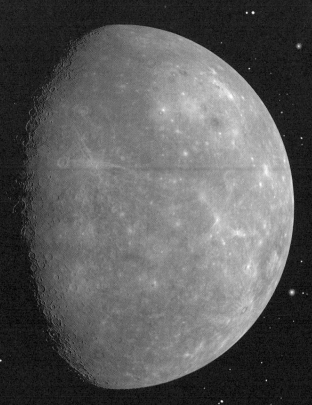

Mercury is the smallest planet in the Solar System and is the closest to the Sun. Its temperature varies from 425°C (800°F) by day to -75°C (-100 °F) at night.

Order and size of the planets in the Solar System:

Mercury
↓

* **God of speed** Mercury is the fastest planet, orbiting the Sun in just three months. It is named after the swift-flying messenger of the Roman gods.

* **Eccentric** Mercury has the most eccentric (oval) orbit of all the planets. The size the Sun appears in its sky varies from two to three times its size seen from Earth.

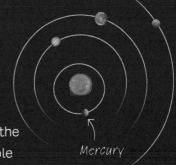

Mercury

* **Long days** Mercury turns so slowly that the time from sunrise to sunset takes a whole Mercurian year (one orbit of the Sun).

* **Rise again** When Mercury is at its closest to the Sun, parts of the planet's surface see it slowly rise halfway, set, then rise again. This is because the pull of the Sun's gravity speeds up Mercury so much that it is orbiting faster than it's turning.

* **Craters** Mercury has no atmosphere to protect it, so it's covered in craters. Most date from four billion years ago when space rocks battered its surface.

The pale brown area on this photo of Mercury is Caloris Basin, a huge crater.

MERCURY FACTS

Diameter: 4,880km (3,032 miles)

Day (dawn to dawn): 175.9 Earth days

Year (one orbit): 88 Earth days

Distance from Sun: 58 million km (36 million miles)

Moons: none

Gravity: 38% Earth

Adjective: Mercurian

Symbol: ☿

Venus

The planet Venus is the brightest light in the sky after the Moon. Its surface is veiled in creamy clouds of carbon dioxide gas.

Order and size of the planets in the Solar System:

Venus
↓

Bright beauty Venus can only be seen from Earth near sunrise or sunset. The Ancient Greeks thought it was two stars: the Morning and Evening Stars. Later, they named it after their goddess of love, Aphrodite, known to the Romans as Venus.

★ **Terrible twin** Venus is the nearest planet to Earth, and close in size. But where our world is wet and welcoming, Venus is a fiery volcanic desert with an atmosphere so dense and heavy it could crush a car.

This is the probe Venus Express.
In 2006, it discovered lightning on Venus.

★ **Back spin** Venus spins in the opposite direction to its orbit, so the Sun rises in the west and sets in the east — although you wouldn't see it through the fog. Scientists think that a planet may have crashed into it and knocked it upside down.

★ **Heavy snowfall** Venus is so hot that heavy metals such as lead turn to gas, then cool and fall on its mountains as metallic snow.

The surface of Venus is strewn with dead volcanoes and shrouded in poisonous fog.

VENUS FACTS

Moons: none

Diameter: 12,100km (7,519 miles)

Gravity: 91% Earth

Day (dawn to dawn): 116.8 Earth days

Adjective: Venusian

Year (one orbit): 224.7 Earth days

Symbol: ♀

Distance from Sun: 108 million km (67 million miles)

Planet Earth

Earth is a rocky planet, the third from the Sun.
Its most striking features are the water that
covers 70% of its surface, and the greenery
and life that water makes possible.

Order and size of the planets in the Solar System:

Earth
↓

* **No place like home** While Mars is frozen, and Venus is boiling, Earth is just the right distance from the Sun to allow plenty of water to exist as a liquid on its surface.

* **Good atmosphere** An atmosphere is a layer of gases around a planet. Earth's atmosphere is just 11—17km (7—11 miles) high. 78% is nitrogen gas. 21% is oxygen, which living things need. The rest is moisture and traces of other gases.

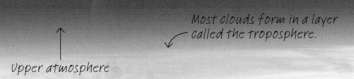

Moon

Most clouds form in a layer called the troposphere.

↑

Upper atmosphere

* **Globe-ish** The Earth is not a perfect sphere, but slightly flattened, so that it measures 42.7km (26.5 miles) more around its equator (east-west) than around its Poles (north-south).

* **Hold tight!** Our planet spins at 1,674kph (1,040mph) at its equator, and it orbits the Sun at 108,000kph (67,000mph).

* **Seasons** Earth is tilted at an angle of 23.5° as it spins. This means that its regions receive varying amounts of direct sunlight during a year, creating seasons. Venus and Mercury have little or no tilt, so they don't have seasons.

EARTH FACTS	Moons: 1
Diameter: 12,742km (7,918 miles)	Inhabitant: Earthling, Terran
Day (dawn to dawn): 24 hours	Adjective: terrestrial
Year (one orbit): 365.256 days	Symbol: ⊕
Distance from Sun: 150 million km (93 million miles)	

The Moon

Size compared to Earth

Earth's only natural satellite, the Moon, is about the size of Australia. It has dark plains called seas or *maria*, and pale highlands known as *terrae*. The bright spots are large craters.

* **Face to face** The Moon takes the same amount of time to spin around as it does to circle the Earth, so it always has the same side facing us. Its far side has many craters and few seas.

* **Phases** As the Moon orbits Earth, one half is always sunlit, but the part we see waxes (grows) and wanes (shrinks) in various phases (stages), seen here as from the northern hemisphere:

New moon   Waxing crescent   First quarter   Waxing gibbous   Full moon   Waning gibbous   Last quarter   Waning crescent

* **Upside down?** A northern visitor to the southern hemisphere would see the Moon 'upside down' — and on its side at the equator.

A waning crescent moon over the equator

* **The Man in the Moon** An old European tradition sees a man's shape in the Moon's dark seas. He carries a bundle of sticks and a lantern, has a small dog, and stands beside a big thorn bush.

MOON FACTS	
	Manned missions: six
Diameter: 3,474km (2,159 miles)	**Gravity:** 17% Earth
Day: 29.5 Earth days	**Adjective:** lunar
Year: 27 Earth days	**Symbol:** ☽
Distance from Earth: 384,403km (238,857 miles)	

To the Moon

Astronaut Buzz Aldrin was the second person on the Moon. Neil Armstrong and the US flag are reflected in his gold-plated visor.

The Eagle's landing On July 20, 1969, *Apollo 11* astronauts Neil Armstrong and Buzz Aldrin became the first men on the Moon. Their landing craft, *Eagle*, overshot its planned site, but Armstrong managed to pilot it across risky terrain to its historic touchdown.

Buzz Aldrin climbs down onto the Moon's surface.

* **Moon shot** At age 47, Project Mercury astronaut Alan Shepard flew to the Moon on *Apollo 14*, becoming the oldest moonwalker — and the first man to play golf on the Moon.

Alan Shepard

* **Be prepared** Eleven of the twelve astronauts who walked on the Moon were former Boy Scouts.

* **Believe it or not** The maiden name of Buzz Aldrin's mother, Marion, was Moon.

MORE MOON MISSION MILESTONES

1959: *Luna-2* (Russia) — 1st probe to crash-land on the Moon

1966: *Luna-9* — 1st controlled landing, sent back photographs

1966: *Luna-10* — 1st probe to enter the Moon's orbit

1968: *Apollo 8* (USA) — 1st manned spacecraft to orbit the Moon

Mars

Valles Marineris

Mars's huge canyon Valles Marineris is
4,000km (2,500 miles) long, stretching
a fifth of the way around the planet.

Order and size of the planets in the Solar System:

Mars
↓

★ **Red planet** Mars was named in ancient times after the Roman god of war. Nicknamed the Red Planet, it is covered with a layer of rusty iron oxide dust and glows orange-red in the sky.

Phobos

Deimos

★ **Fear and Dread** Mars has a rounded moon called Phobos and a smaller, potato-shaped one called Deimos. They were named after the sons of Ares, the Greek god of war. Their names mean Fear and Dread.

★ **Olympus Mons** Named after Mount Olympus in Greece, this Martian volcano is 27km (17 miles) high: nearly three times as high as the tallest mountain on Earth.

★ **Desert views** The surface of Mars has been extensively mapped and photographed by satellites and robot rovers. The image below was taken by NASA's *Spirit* rover.

MARS FACTS

Diameter: 6,794km (4,222 miles)	**Moons:** two
Day (dawn to dawn): 24 Earth hrs, 42 mins	**Gravity:** 38% Earth
Year (one orbit): 687 Earth days	**Adjective:** Martian
Distance from Sun: 228 million km (142 million miles)	**Symbol:** ♂

Jupiter

Jupiter is the largest planet in the Solar System,
ten times as wide as Earth. Its swirling atmosphere
is striped with pale 'zones' and darker 'bands'.

Order and size of the planets in the Solar System:

Jupiter
↓

* **King of the planets** Jupiter is the brightest of the planets in the night sky. (Venus only appears near dawn or dusk.) It was named by the Romans after the king of the gods.

* **Gas giant** Jupiter is called a gas giant, but most of its insides are in fact liquid. The hydrogen and helium that make it up are pressed by the weight of its atmosphere into liquid form. Jupiter has no definite outer surface: the liquid blends gradually into a thick atmosphere of ammonia gas. Deep inside is a rocky core.

* **Great Red Spot** Jupiter spins over twice as quickly as Earth, creating winds of up to 560kph (350mph). Its Great Red Spot is a massive hurricane that has lasted many centuries because Jupiter, unlike Earth, has no land to slow it down.

Two Earths could fit inside Jupiter's Great Red Spot.

* **Comet catcher** The pull of giant Jupiter's gravity has given it the largest collection of moons in the Solar System. It also attracts or knocks away passing comets, protecting Earth from violent impacts.

JUPITER FACTS

Diameter: 142,984km (88,846 miles)	**Moons:** at least 67
Day (dawn to dawn): 9 Earth hrs, 56 mins	**Gravity:** 253% Earth
Year (one orbit): 11.9 Earth years	**Adjective:** Jovian
Distance from Sun: 778 million km (483 million miles)	**Symbol:** ♃

Jupiter's moons

Jupiter has at least 67 moons. The largest four
are called the Galilean moons. This photo, taken
by a space probe called *Cassini*, shows Io, the
third largest, casting a shadow onto its surface.

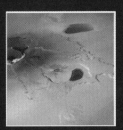
Lava flowing on Io

✳ Io Jupiter's gravity pulls at this moon, warping its rocky surface. The friction heats its insides, forming volcanoes that erupt nearly all the time. In 2007, a probe called Galileo saw lava (hot liquid rock) on Io.

Volcanic Io

✳ Ganymede Larger than Mercury, this is the Solar System's biggest moon. If it orbited the Sun, it would be classed as a planet.

Planet-sized Ganymede

✳ Europa The surface of this icy moon cracks and refreezes as it is affected by Jupiter's gravity. Beneath may lie deep, salty oceans and perhaps even alien sealife.

Does life lurk in Europa's oceans?

✳ Callisto Jupiter's second largest moon is too far out to be strongly altered by its gravity. Its surface hasn't changed since it was formed, except as a result of meteor strikes. Callisto is the most cratered object in the Solar System.

Cratered Callisto

MORE FACTS ABOUT JUPITER'S MOONS

Largest: Ganymede, diameter: 5,268km (3,273 miles)

Smallest: S/2003 J 12, diameter 1km (0.6 miles)

Innermost: Metis, distance 128,000km (80,000 miles)

Outermost: S/2003 J 2, distance 30 million km (18.6 million miles)

Saturn

This is the Solar System's second largest planet. It is surrounded by rings made up of pieces of ice, from tiny specks to chunks the size of a small car. These vast rings are, incredibly, just 10m (30ft) thick.

Order and size of the planets in the Solar System:

Saturn
↓

* **Ring origins** Saturn's rings may have been created when a big, icy moon tried to form too close to the planet and fell into it, shedding its outer layers on the way. These remains gradually settled into the flat rings we see today.

D Ring*   C Ring*   B Ring   Cassini Division   A Ring   Encke Gap

(*dark rings)

* **Lightweight** The gas giant Saturn is the least dense planet in the Solar System. If a large enough ocean could be found, Saturn would float in it.

* **Bulging waistline** Saturn spins so rapidly that it has a slightly flattened shape, bulging out 10% more around its middle.

* **Stormy Saturn** Saturn has winds with speeds of up to 1,800kph (1,118mph), and huge lightning storms that last for months.

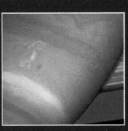

The 2004 `Dragon Storm' on Saturn had lightning 1,000 times stronger than Earth.

SATURN FACTS

Diameter: 120,536km (74,898 miles)	**Moons:** at least 62
Day (dawn to dawn): 10 Earth hrs, 39 mins	**Gravity:** 91% Earth
Year (one orbit): 29.5 Earth years	**Adjective:** Saturnian
Distance from Sun: 1,427 million km (887 million miles)	**Symbol:** ♄

Saturn's moons

Oil and gas are precious fuels on Earth, but on Saturn's largest moon, Titan, liquid gas falls as rain. The *Cassini* probe has taken pictures of lakes and seas of dark, oily chemicals.

* **Titan** The largest moon
in the Solar System after Jupiter's
Ganymede, Titan is the only place outside Earth known to have
liquid lakes and seas. Some scientists say its oily chemicals may
be complex enough for simple alien life to have developed there.

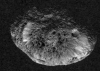

* **Hyperion** This oddball, burger-shaped moon has
so many craters it looks like a sponge. Its shape,
along with Saturn and Titan's gravity pulling at it,
make it twist and wobble in an unpredictable way.

* **Enceladus** This white moon has four
'tiger stripe' cracks near its South Pole.
They contain ice fountains which, when
they erupt, spray icy particles 100km
(60 miles) above the surface.

* **Mimas** Nicknamed the Death Star
moon because of its likeness to the
space station in *Star Wars*, little Mimas
has a crater nearly a third of its width.

* **Shepherd moons** These little moons orbit between Saturn's
rings, or at their edges, 'herding' together the icy chunks that
make up the rings, and whipping them into complicated patterns.

FACTS ABOUT SATURN'S MOONS

Pan: Saturn's closest moon, orbits in the Encke gap in its 'A Ring'

Iapetus: this two-tone moon is shaped like a walnut shell

Phoebe: orbits 13 million km (8 million miles) away from Saturn

Moonlets: hundreds of mini-moons, just 100m (328ft) wide

Uranus

The pale blue face of Uranus, the third largest
planet, comes from clouds of frozen methane.
It is named after the Greek god of the sky.

Order and size of the planets in the Solar System:

Uranus
↓

* **George's star** Uranus was the first planet to be found through a telescope, by William Herschel in 1781. At first, he named it *Georgium Sidus* (George's Star) after British King George III, but other astronomers wanted it to be named after a god.

* **Rings** Uranus has rings made of frozen methane. They are much fainter than Saturn's, but are visible in the photo below.

* **Rolling along** Like Venus, Uranus spins from east to west, but is tilted on its side. It was probably knocked sideways by another planet early in its life.

* **Changing seasons** Uranus's steep tilt and long orbit give it highly contrasting seasons that last 21 Earth years. When a probe took a photo of Uranus in 1977, it was in its calm autumn. A 2003 photo (right) shows late winter clouds and bright storms.

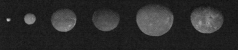

Uranus's largest moons, in shadow. From left to right: Puck, Miranda, Ariel, Umbriel, Titania and Oberon

* **Dramatic moons** The moons of Uranus are named after characters from plays and poems by Shakespeare and Alexander Pope.

URANUS FACTS

Diameter: 51,118km (31,763 miles)	**Moons:** 27
Day (dawn to dawn): 17 Earth hrs, 14 mins	**Gravity:** 89% Earth
Year (one orbit): 84 Earth years	**Adjective:** Uranian
Distance from Sun: 2,871 million km (1,784 million miles)	**Symbol:** ♅

Neptune

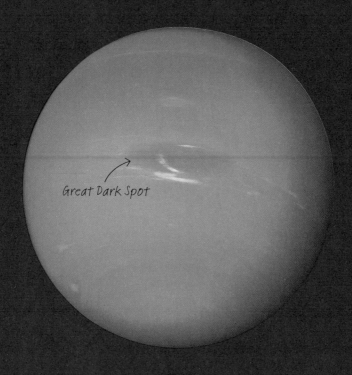

Great Dark Spot

The eighth planet from the Sun is Neptune,
named after the Roman god of the sea. Its
deep blue comes from a methane atmosphere.

Order and size of the planets in the Solar System:

Neptune

High winds The gas giant Neptune has the fastest winds in the Solar System, reaching speeds of 2,100kph (1,300mph).

* **Changing spots** Like Jupiter, Neptune has storms that rage for years. A storm called the Great Dark Spot (see page 28), was photographed by the *Voyager 2* probe in 1989. It had gone by 1994, but a new 'Northern' Great Dark Spot soon appeared.

* **Triton** Neptune's largest moon, Triton, orbits it in the opposite direction to which the planet spins. Experts think it was once a dwarf planet in the Kuiper Belt, but was pulled in by Neptune's gravity.

Triton

* **Ice geysers** Triton is made mainly of frozen nitrogen. Warmth from the distant Sun reaches beneath its surface, melting the ice until it erupts in huge plumes of nitrogen gas.

Ice fountain on Triton

NEPTUNE FACTS

Moons: 14

Diameter: 49,528km (30,755 miles)

Gravity: 114% Earth

Day (dawn to dawn): 16 Earth hrs, 7 mins

Adjective: Neptunian

Year (one orbit): 165 Earth years

Symbol: ♆

Distance from Sun: 4,498 million km (2,795 million miles)

Pluto and the dwarf planets

Pluto's largest moon, Charon

This is NASA's New Horizons probe. It is due to reach Pluto in 2015.

Pluto, pictured here, is one of the largest of the dwarf planets. These are mostly small, icy objects that orbit the Sun in a region called the Kuiper Belt in the outer limits of the Solar System.

* **Pluto** Pluto is so far away from the Sun, it takes 248 years to orbit it, and can be as cold as -240°C (-400°F). Found in 1930 by US astronomer Clyde Tombaugh, Pluto was named after the Roman god of the dead, and was known as the ninth planet.

* **QB1** In 1992, another large object (named QB1) was found in the same area as Pluto, the first of hundreds of such objects now known to orbit beyond Neptune, in what is called the Kuiper Belt.

* **Sedna** This object, discovered in 2003, orbits up to 144 billion km (90 billion miles) away, making it the most distant thing we know of in the Solar System.

* **Eris** In 2005, an object that may be larger than Pluto was found. It started arguments about what 'planet' means, and was named after Eris, the Greek goddess of conflict.

Sun

Sedna

* **The dwarfs** In 2006, astronomers decided that space objects such as Pluto and Eris should be called dwarf planets. Although they're big enough to be round like a planet, they're too small to drive most objects out of their orbits.

MORE DWARF PLANETS (* = to be confirmed)

Makemake: 1,420km (882 miles) wide, named after Polynesian god

Haumea: 1,960km (1,218 miles) long, named after Hawaiian goddess

Ceres: 975km (606 miles) wide, only dwarf planet in Asteroid Belt

*****Sedna:** 1,600km (994 miles) wide, named after Inuit sea goddess

Index

Acknowledgements

p2 NASA, SOHO (ESA/NASA); p3 NASA; p4-5 SOHO (ESA/NASA); p6 NASA/MESSENGER/
Prockter; p7 (b) NASA/MESSENGER; p8, Raw data: NASA/JPL, image processing & panorama
by Mattias Malmer; p9 (t) ESA (b) NASA; p10 NASA's Earth Observatory; p11 NASA; p12 Moon
NASA/JPL Earth NASA/GSFC SVS; p13: (t) NASA/JPL (b) Moon NASA/JPL; p14, p15 NASA; p16
NASA/Viking 1; p17 NASA; p18 NASA/JPL/University of Arizona; p19 NASA/Voyager 2/PDS/
NSSDC/Bjorn Jonsson; p20 NASA/JPL/UA; p21 (tl) NASA/JPL/Galileo (tr) NASA/JPL/UA (ml)
NASA/JPL (mr, bl) NASA/JPL/DLR; p22, p23 NASA/JPL/Space Science Institute; p24 © Karl
Kofoed; p25 (tr, mr, bl) NASA/JPL/SSI (ml) NASA/JPL/SSI/Gordan Ugarkovic; p26NASA/JPL; p27
(mr) NASA/ESA/Erich Karkoschka, UA (bl) NASA/JPL (bm) NASA/Ted Stryk; p28 NASA/JPL; p29
(ml) NASA/JPL/USGS (b) David A. Hardy/SPL;p30 NASA/JHUAPL/SRI; p31 NASA/JPL-Caltech

Edited by Rachel Firth   Photoshop: Mike Olley   Cover design: Nelupa Hussain